MILLIONAIRE BUSINESS SECRETS

THE REAL BEGINNERS GUIDE TO STARTING A BUSINESS

NOELLE RANDALL,
MPS, MBA

Copyright © 2021 by Noelle Randall

All rights reserved. In accordance with the U.S. Copyright Act of 1976, the scanning, uploading, and electronic sharing of any part of this book without the permission of the publisher constitute unlawful piracy and theft of the author's intellectual property. If you would like to use material from the book (other than for review purposes), prior written permission must be obtained by contacting the publisher at books@waltonpublishinghouse.com Reviewers may quote brief passages in reviews.

Walton Publishing House Houston, Texas
www.waltonpublishinghouse.com

Printed in the United States of America

The advice found within may not be suitable for every individual. This work is purchased with the understanding that neither the author nor the publisher is held responsible for any results. Neither author nor publisher assumes responsibility for errors, omissions, or contrary interpretations of the subject matter herein. Any perceived disparagement of an individual or organization is a misinterpretation.

Brand and product names mentioned are trademarks that belong solely to their respective owners. Library of Congress Cataloging-in-Publication Data under

ISBN: 978-1-953993-14-4 (Paperback)

ISBN: 978-1-953993-15-1 (Digital/ Ebook)

CONTENTS

Introduction 5

Chapter One:
Are You Ready? 8

Chapter Two:
What's Your Vision? 18

Chapter Three:
What Business Suits You? 26

Chapter Four:
Become an Expert in Your Industry 42

Chapter Five:
Where Are Your Customers? 55

Chapter Six:
Learn, Do & Teach 62

Chapter Seven:
Growing a Million Dollar Brand 74

Chapter Eight:
Get Your Business Funded 82

Chapter Nine:
The Millionaire Mindset 90

Chapter Ten:
To Your Success 103

Acknowledgement 108

About the Author 109

Connect with Noelle 112

DEDICATION

This book is dedicated to anyone experiencing the fear of letting go of your 9-5 job. I know that feeling all too well. I hope this book will inspire you to take a leap of faith, become your own boss and own your own time.

Thank you!

INTRODUCTION

Hello Future Millionaire,

If you have been following me on the journey to success, you probably know that my mission is to help you become a millionaire. I believe everyone should have the opportunity to experience a life that brings them fulfillment and pleasure. I also believe that everyone deserves a shot at creating a financial legacy for their family. So let me make this a bit more personal. My friend, I want you to experience what it feels like to achieve millionaire status.

Becoming a millionaire is easier than you think. You may be saying, of course, you would feel that way; you're already a millionaire. Yes, it's true, I am a millionaire. But, it's also true that I started from my parents' basement, and I had to put one foot in front of the other, show up consistently, have a vision, and do the work. In other words, nothing was handed to me. I didn't have rich family members to pass on a dynasty to me. I didn't have rich friends who could have loaned me the money for my business. And here I am today, showing you by my personal story that it is possible. And guess what? If you apply what I teach you, you can also have the same success.

In this book, we will dive into the tools you need to attain the success you deserve. Real estate ignited and catapulted me into the success you see today, but I had a passion for business even before I got into real estate. I had tried my hand at multiple businesses, and I was determined to keep going until something worked out for me. This is the drive and passion that you, as an entrepreneur, must also possess.

If I had the roadmap to create a successful business like the one that I am passing on to you, I would have reached millionaire status much sooner. Please know that I am holding nothing back from you. I realize the sooner you understand and apply these concepts, the sooner you will be on your way to success.

Did you know that you can start building a business with an empty bank account and still find success? That's right! You don't need to have all the resources in place or have a ton of money. Likewise, you don't need to have the best credit or have many contacts, leads, and prospects before you begin.

Every business that was created did not exist before its creation. You get to create the business that you want, and you get to do it your way. Now is a good time for you to think about the goals you have for your life. Keeping a clear vision in front of you will keep you motivated and focused as you build your million-dollar business.

There are so many benefits to being a business owner. As a business owner and entrepreneur, I can tell you that I get to own my time. And more importantly, I get to set my own income limits. These are important things about being an entrepreneur, because if you set your business up correctly, it can provide you with more income than you've ever desired. You can own your own time because you will not be working too many hours while working for someone else. And more importantly, you can work with people that you want to work with. Does this seem promising to you? I hope so! Because the sooner you become excited about your future, the sooner you will see it manifest in your life.

I wrote this book with you in mind. I want you to start a business you love. I want you to find success – this year! It is time out for the excuses and playing small and time for you to take action. It's time for you to take charge of your life.

Are you ready? Let's go!

To Your Success,
Noelle

Learn the tools and experience NOELLE RANDALL live or virtual at www.NoelleRandallEvents.com. Use code "BMS" to save 50% on tickets

CHAPTER ONE:
ARE YOU READY?

"If you really look closely, most overnight successes took a long time."
- Steve Jobs

ARE YOU READY?

It takes a lot of work to become a millionaire. There I said it! Now that we have gotten that out of the way, I want to tell you that even though building a million-dollar business is hard work – it gets easier once you have the blueprint for success. I call this blueprint the *Grow Your Wealth Blueprint (GYWB)*. The *GYWB* is the one system that I adopted in my real estate business that has garnered me the income to reach multi-millionaire status in just a few short years. Like you, I once found myself seeking answers and wanting to know how I would become the millionaire that I knew I was destined to be. As I sat in my parents' basement, even though I had lost everything, I never stopped dreaming and believing in myself.

I want to teach you what I have learned from my mentors, what I have learned through hands-on experience, and countless hours of personal development. But first, I want to applaud you for taking control of your future by reading this book. The ideas you have for your business are just the beginning of something amazing. In fact, everything great first began as an idea. This sounds simple, right? Sure, it does, but it's also so simple that you'll find yourself frustrated with where you are at this point in your life if you don't accept it. So let me break this down a bit further.

Where you are right now is exactly where you need to be. It doesn't matter how you landed there or how long you've been there; it only matters what happens from here. I say that for two reasons. The first is, there is something you need to learn in your current state that will help you on your road to making millions. Secondly, there is a concept, system, or habit you need to master in order to create the business and life you deserve. Unfortunately, many entrepreneurs find themselves stuck somewhere between those two levels.

But it's honestly a good place to be – or should I say pass through. If you stay in either one of those levels for too long, you will never see the success you deserve. On the contrary, if you apply the lessons you will learn in level one coupled with the systems in level two, you will reach your ultimate success level. So again, let me reiterate this – where you are right now is exactly where you should be. Where you go from here is entirely up to you. You have control and responsibility for your life choices.

Before we dive in too deep, from this point forward I want you to forget everything you think you know about becoming a successful entrepreneur. That's right! I want you to remove the thoughts of *how you've always done it*. I want you to remove from your memory bank the things your unsuccessful family members, colleagues, or best friends from high school taught you. I even want you to forget what you learned in college and post-graduate school. As well-meaning as your influences may have been, the truth is they can't help you reach a level in life they've never attained for themselves. You can't teach someone how to do something you've never accomplished repeatedly.

I also want you to take this time to think about where you want to go from here. Reflect on why you want to start your business and what type of legacy you want to leave. Starting a business for me was about owning my own time and creating a financial legacy for my family. I found little time to enjoy life while holding down a full-time job and performing the duties of a wife and a mother. I wanted to spend time with those that I loved the most. However, many times I found myself working late hours and spending long hours on the road. It really bothered me when my kids would say things like, "you're always working" or "you're always busy." They would joke about how much I traveled or joke about me missing their games. After a while, I started to really see the substance behind the jokes. I didn't want to be the parent that missed the games or didn't know any of my children's friends. Finally, the reality hit, and I started listening and realizing that I was working way too hard for the money and didn't feel fulfilled. I knew I had to do something different. Even knowing this and feeling this strong conviction, I kept going to work every day, convincing myself that it was what my family needed. *We need the money,* I told myself.

I have to confess that I should have left my 9-5 job long before I did. I am ashamed to say that I allowed fear to keep me from taking the leap. One day, I built enough courage to do it finally. After I quit my job, things were going well for the first month or two, and like any new entrepreneur, I felt free and excited about finally taking the leap. By the third month, the reality of what I had done kicked in, and I started to panic. An overwhelming fear set in, I began questioning my decision, and I worried about how I would make it. I started doubting myself, and I was affected by Imposter Syndrome.

According to the Harvard Business Review, " Imposter syndrome[1] can be defined as a collection of feelings of inadequacy that persist despite evident success. 'Imposters' suffer from chronic self-doubt and a sense of intellectual fraudulence that override any feelings of success or external proof of their competence." This describes how I felt when I questioned

---

1   [Oxford English Dictionary] (n.d.} Imposter Syndrome. Retrieved June 06, 2021, from Oxford Languages

my decision. *Only a crazy person would leave a six-figure salaried job with a steady paycheck, I reasoned.* It was thoughts like this that allowed fear to cause me to second guess myself.

Before I knew it, I was caught in a negative mental trap, and it was exhausting. I started thinking, *what if I can't make the money again? What if one of my clients cancels? What if I fall flat on my face?* The toxic thoughts filled my mind until finally, I convinced myself to return to Corporate America. Yes, you read that correctly. After taking the leap, I panicked and later returned to work with my tail between my legs. Knowing what I know now, if I would have learned the Grow Your Wealth Blueprint, I could have created a business that I loved sooner. I was the victim of bad mental programming.

Bad mental programming is something many entrepreneurs on the journey to success will need to overcome and conquer. The panic attacks that I suffered were a product of my unstable mind – there was no truth to substantiate how I felt. It was just me allowing negative thought patterns to crowd my mind because none of it happened. Bad mental programming is prevalent everywhere. It's the negative things we think about ourselves or even what others say about us that feed the programming. It is the lies we tell ourselves that talk us out of the opportunities in our life that are waiting for us to show up. It includes the limiting beliefs that convince you that the real estate market is oversaturated or there is a shortage of money. I have repeatedly said it, and I will continue to say it, there is more than enough money for all of us. But, you will first need to believe it before you can manifest the countless number of opportunities available. Let that sink in for a moment. ***There is more than enough for you.***

Reprogram Your Thinking

One of the most significant pieces of advice I can give on your road to making millions is to re-program your thinking. Whatever you think about, you will manifest. When I was having those panic attacks about failing, I didn't realize how important my mental state was and how it was limiting my ability to attract wealth. Over time, I learned that our thoughts become things. So, if you want something to become real and tangible, meditate on it often. This works in both the positive and negative aspects of your life. For example, if you want to stay broke, keep telling yourself that you can't afford things. But, as I know you do, if you want to make millions of dollars, keep telling yourself that you will be a millionaire. It's as simple as a mindset shift.

Overcoming Limiting Beliefs

I mention overcoming limiting beliefs quite a bit as I teach and coach others. I truly believe that the battle of the mind will be the biggest and hardest battle you will need to overcome to build a million-dollar business. Thinking too small was one of my limiting beliefs. When I first started, I wanted to make a million dollars a year. I thought it would take me over ten or more years to see this type of success. That was another limiting belief. I believed that in order for a person to increase their revenue, they would need to do it to scale or at a reasonable level. For instance, if you make $400,000 one year, then you're probably only going to make $500,000 or $600,000 the following year. I never really thought that you could go from $400,000 a year to $4,000,000 to $40,000,000 to $400,000,000. I didn't think that I could literally make ten times my income. I didn't even think that was possible until I saw people doing it. I was trained in Corporate America, where the raises and bonuses were on a scale. You could never really jump into a different income bracket in your annual salary unless you were promoted to a higher position or received a bonus. It was honestly difficult for me to accept that there were no ceilings to how much money I could make in one year. Today, I can tell you that you must release the limiting beliefs to be successful in business. Most people don't really realize how big you can make it in business.

Another limiting belief that many people have when considering starting a business is that they need a certificate or a license for every business they want to start; I was guilty of this as well. I thought I had to follow an extensive checklist in order to be valued in the marketplace as an expert. I had all these silly rules in my mind, but ***I soon learned there are no rules to making money.*** You can be 22 years old and have a $55 million fund. I've met a guy that had one. Or you can be bankrupt and make $3.6 million in six hours.

In order to overcome my limiting beliefs, I had to do a lot of inner work. I incorporated personal development, read books, and went to seminars. I had a spiritual awakening as well. I got baptized, I started going to church, I walked on hot coals, I walked on glass, and I had to face my fears. I had to get stronger and grow. I had to toughen up because I thought it was hard to make money. I just could not get it. Even when I started earning more money and attaining success, I always thought someone would take it away or something terrible was going to happen.

There was so much inner work I needed to do to get rid of the fears – but I did it. And before long, I started believing in myself and becoming more confident. Can I confess that even the things that I share with my audience and write in my books resulted from me building my confidence. It's true! I am generally a private person, and it took me being vulnerable to share my setbacks and failures to grow my brand to where it is today. It took me confessing that I don't always have it together.

> Millionaire Secret #1- On your road to millions, you must reprogram your thinking. Whatever you think about, you will manifest.

Chapter Recap

- One of the biggest pieces of advice I can give on your road to making millions is to reprogram your thinking. Whatever you think about, you will manifest.
- You cannot build a million-dollar business without a clear vision and action steps.
- Reflect on why you want to start your business and what type of legacy you want to leave.
- To build a million-dollar business, the battle of the mind will be the biggest and hardest battle you will need to overcome.
- There are no rules to making money.

Notes:

CHAPTER TWO:
WHAT'S YOUR VISION?

"Vision is not just a picture of what could be; it is an appeal to our better selves, a call to become something more.
- Rosabeth Moss Kanter"

WHAT'S YOUR VISION?

When I decided to become an Entrepreneur, I had to first start with a clear vision; I am a true visionary. I can come up with an idea that no one in the room understands or is able to see, and that is okay with me. Being a visionary means, you can see things before it's built. It means that you can see a whole project when there's just dirt there. I understand every aspect of business; I can see an empty field and see a future Walmart. I can see the parking lines and the cars parked in front of the store. I can see the people coming in, and I can see where the Chick-Fil-A will be located. I can see the other stores in the strip mall. I can see all of it while looking at an empty field. That's the skill of a visionary, and you have to be able to do the exact same thing if you want to be a millionaire. You must be able to see things that are not there. You have to be able to create from something that does not exist. In order to make the incredible, you have to be able to see things that do not exist.

The vision you have for your life may seem intimidating at first. I am sure most successful entrepreneurs have questioned if they had what it took to manifest the vision they saw for themselves. However, many of those same successful entrepreneurs will tell you it all started with a dream. Your vision is the path to your future that shows you there is still more for you to do. Your vision solidifies that there is more for you to learn and more for you to experience. A vision is a personal message that there is more to your life than what you've lived.

> **Millionaire Secret #2 - You cannot build a million-dollar business without a clear vision and action steps.**

"Imagination is everything. It is the preview of life's coming attractions."
- Albert Einstein

As you begin your path to millionaire status, I want you to take the time to write your vision down and review it often. As an entrepreneur, your vision will guide you on the right path and lead you to the right people. It will also keep you focused on the right things and the actions you need to take to bring about results. Your mental GPS will direct you to where your profitable business, the right connections, the required mentorship, and the wealth of knowledge that is waiting for you.

Once you have your vision in place, you will need to set your goals. Your goals are bite-sized action steps that lead you to your vision. Goal setting is essential for anyone looking to take the leap from a traditional job to a full-time entrepreneur. For example, when I decided I wanted to quit my job and work for myself full-time, I made my "escape plan" to determine when I would resign. Yes, that's really what I called it. I wrote down the day that I was going to resign from my job – then I reverse engineered a plan to take the leap. It took me only a year to orchestrate and implement that plan. With the tools I teach today, it will most likely not take you that long. With the right business structure, a stable source of income, and business credit, it probably won't take you longer than six months.

WHAT'S YOUR VISION?

I would even challenge you by saying the reason you haven't quit your job yet is because of the wrong mindset, your lack of vision and failure to set goals. Because the truth of the matter is, if somebody is paying you $50,000, $60,000, or $80,000 a year or more, then you can make that on your own unequivocally. I just believe that. Think about it. If somebody else is willing to pay you that amount per year, you are bringing value to someone else's business. With the right systems, don't you think you can at least make double that on your own? I think you can.

If you are open to receive and apply the knowledge, you will find that success will be knocking down your door – this is no exaggeration. Once I learned the right systems and committed to doing the work, I realized there was no feat I couldn't achieve. This also applies to building your million-dollar business. There is a system to becoming a leader in your industry and taking your rightful place as a wealth magnet. There is a system to accumulate wealth and seamlessly create multiple streams of income. Learning this system changed the trajectory of me and my family's life. I am so grateful for the day I became a student of the system. Today, I have mastered this system, and I will be sharing my secrets with you throughout this book.

> Millionaire Secret #3 - Your mental state is the foundation of everything you do.

If you listen to my teachings or have read my books, you know this is something I will continue to say repeatedly. I understand how the right mental state shifted my life. In fact, being in the right mental state will help you reach your goals in record time. Your mental state is the foundation of everything you will do. Now

I am going to say something here that may sound a bit crazy. If you want to build a million-dollar business, forget everything you think you know about running a business, making money, marketing, securing customers, and anything else that makes you believe "oh, I know that already." To be successful in business, you must start with a clean mental slate. Until you hit your first million-dollar milestone, you are a student, and after you hit it, you're still a student. Please allow me to repeat that. You are a student; this is not to belittle you. I hope you know that is not something I would ever do to you. But I need to take you back to where I began to help you understand the journey. In life, you always want to remain a student. Let me tell you why:

- Being a student allows you to make mistakes.
- Being a student allows you the freedom to ask questions without the fear of appearing stupid.
- Being a student allows you to create an environment of growth and learning.

Do you understand where I am going with this? Does it make sense to you when you look at it from that perspective?

_____

_____

_____

_____

_____

_____

_____

I made big mistakes and lost the most money when I attempted to skip over the student level and slide right into being the "expert." There is a story that I tell my audience about how I invested in an antique fixer-upper without having a complete understanding of what I was doing. Had I applied my own words and remained a student, I wouldn't have lost so much money. Instead, the project was a complete flop. Over time I learned the hard way that I needed to reprogram myself. I needed to do some mindset work: journaling, reciting affirmations, and meditation to get rid of all of that anxiety that depressed me.

This is my big secret to success; I first began with a mental overhaul. I created some healthy habits and started a consistent daily routine. I changed everything about me, and I started on the inside first. This is what it ultimately takes to become a millionaire. This is what it takes to find success in your industry. There is no shortcut to this.

Chapter Recap:

- Being a visionary means, you can see things before it's built.
- If you want to become a millionaire, you must be a visionary.
- As an entrepreneur, your vision will guide you on the right path and lead you to the right people. It will also keep you focused on the right things and the actions you need to take to bring about results.
- Once you have your vision in place, you will need to set your goals. Your goals are bite-sized action steps that lead you to your vision.
- Until you hit your first million-dollar milestone, you are a student, and after you hit it – you're still a student.

WHAT'S YOUR VISION?

Notes:

CHAPTER THREE:
WHAT BUSINESS SUITS YOU?

"All our dreams can come true, if we have the courage to pursue them."
– Walt Disney.

Today, I am widely known for my real estate business, but many people don't know that I have over six other businesses that bring in over a million dollars each in revenue. I am not telling you this to brag or toot my horn – I am telling you this so you can see that it is possible. What is possible for me is also possible for you. Do you believe that? I desire that by sharing my story, you will be able to see how we all start from the same position and how we all have access to endless possibilities. A successful life awaits you once you are clear about your vision and follow the right systems. I wish I could have snapped my fingers and watched my business elevate from zero to millionaire status overnight, but that's just not the way success works; I had to put in the necessary work.

One of the first questions many entrepreneurs will ask is, how do I know which business is best suited for me? That's an excellent question, and honestly, only a question that you can answer for yourself. I'm a firm believer that there is no wrong business, and there is no business idea that won't work.

Before I started in real estate, I put my hands in all types of businesses, both traditional and multi-level marketing. I wanted to be successful, but I was unsure which vehicle would get me there the fastest. I've sold body wraps with It Works, energy drinks with Thrive, and I've sold detox tea. I also owned a brick-and-mortar hair weave extension shop, which eventually my partner and I transitioned to online sales because it was much more profitable.

I've had some epic failures along the way to making my millions. I can laugh now about the things that did not work out as planned. One of those failures was the mortgage underwriter's course, "Make 75K." I was so excited when I came up with the idea. I was sure this course would put me on the map and open doors to a multiple six figures income. It was my intention in that course to teach people how to become a Mortgage Underwriter. My rationale for naming the course "Make 75K" was that it was a job that paid around $75,000 per year with no college degree required. In my mind, this was a brilliant concept. I could help people earn $75,000 without a college degree. Sadly, it was short-lived because Google considered the domain name suspicious and banned it when I attempted to run ads.

My mortgage processing company was also another business that failed as quickly as it started. One day, while in the middle of a major closing, my business partner was involved in a domestic dispute. This happened during the era when you had to print all of the documents – yes, a long time ago. Because of this situation, my partner landed at the local police precinct, and I spent most of that day trying to get the mortgage closing documents from there. Yes, you read that correctly. Let's just say this wasn't a shining moment for a new business owner. I share these embarrassing moments because I want you to know that I relate to the struggles of an entrepreneur who is building a business. I have had my share of "No, thank you," "We're not interested," "I need to talk to my husband," and "It's not the right time." Although you see me today with over 300,000 YouTube subscribers, it wasn't always like this, trust me.

So, let's backtrack to the initial question, "How do you know what business is best suited for you?" Allow me to give you some direction to help guide you. I always advise my students to lean towards the business they would do, even if no one was paying them. In other words, start a business that you would be willing to work both day and night without any compensation. This may seem contrary to what many business models tell you to do, but I have repeatedly witnessed this model work. If it's something you're passionate about and are willing to work at it consistently for free, you'll make money one day. As a new entrepreneur, you may find yourself working for free before you get paid. If you think otherwise, then you are never ever going to make money. You must know you're not going to get rich overnight. You will need to build a solid rapport, customers that can trust you, and people that can vouch for your services. The true entrepreneur actually provides the service or supplies the product in most cases before they're paid. My philosophy has always been to focus less on the money and focus more on delivering your product or service in the best way possible. But just know that you're not going to do it for free for long because you're bringing value, so people will pay you. You should know that the greater the value, the greater the payout.

"Build your business success around something that you love — something that is inherently and endlessly interesting to you." - Martha Stewart, Businesswoman

What Are You Passionate About?

One of the things you want to do is start thinking about what you want to do each day. I call this your passion, the thing that you love doing. As an entrepreneur, you can do a myriad of things, but what you want to do for your business is going to depend on you. What are your talents? What are your passions? What are some of the things that you enjoy doing? I feel I need to emphasize the importance of doing what you love because most people start a business by saying, "Well, how can I make money?" and that is the absolute wrong question. If you do something you are passionate about, you will stay committed to it.

I have helped entrepreneurs make over half a million dollars a year by selling crystals and rocks. Others have coached people through divorces and helped parents potty trained their kids. You can make money doing anything. Whatever your talent is, trust me, you can make money doing it; it just depends on you. If you don't know what your talent is, I want to encourage you to find out. Here are some other helpful questions to help you decide the type of business you want to pursue.

What is your niche?

What is your story?

How are you going to connect with people so that you can show them your transformation with your product or with your service?

Don't copy what other people are doing. Instead, write down who you are and articulate your story. What is it that you're bringing to the table, and what is it that you can keep doing year after year? Building a million-dollar business is not an endeavor you can dabble in or just do it for a couple of months. Think about what you want to do for the next few years and the rest of your life.

> Millionaire Secret # 4- Focus less on the money and focus more on delivering your product or service in the best way possible.

As a business owner, you should be passionate about your business. Being passionate will help you maintain your stamina and keep your momentum growing. If you are not passionate about your business, then you should probably stay at your full-time job. This may seem harsh, but it's true. Think about it. Why would you leave a steady income only to sit in front of your computer unhappy and discontented? Aside from the money aspect of becoming a business owner, you want to enjoy what you are doing because you'll be spending long hours doing it.

I chose real estate because it was what I loved; I would do it for free. I have always loved looking at houses. I love looking at model homes, and I love how they smell. I love how Home Depot and Lowe's smell. I love how wood smells. I love when things are old and when they are transformed and look brand new. I'm not a professional decorator, but I do have an eye for decor. I am passionate about everything concerning real estate, and it has been a great experience with amazing results. Because of my passion, I am building a real estate empire. If you get into real estate just because of the money, you can be sure that you won't last. In fact, anything you pursue just for the income and not for the love of the opportunity, you will find yourself bored and frustrated, which will, in turn, limit you. As you are thinking about what business to start, spend some quiet time reflecting on the things you are passionate about.

How will you know what's right for you?

You will have a good feeling when a business is right for you. I knew real estate was the right vehicle for me when I started investing in real estate and flipping houses as a side hustle while I still had a full-time job. When you discover the business that is right for you, don't let anyone talk you out of it. If I had a dollar for every time I was encouraged to drop real estate and get a "real job," well, let's just say my millions would have hit much sooner. Being in business is something you will need to learn and grow, and sometimes it will require you to go against the grain. If you are a first-generation entrepreneur in your family, don't be discouraged if you don't receive the support you need. Before long, your success will begin to speak for you, and those family and friends who once talked badly about you will ask you how you did it?

The "Escape" Plan

I mentioned earlier that I devised an escape plan when I wanted to leave my full-time job. If you are still working a corporate job or a full-time job and you want to pursue your business full-time, you will need to create one as well. You should include in the plan when you want to leave your job and how you will take care of your bills. No matter how excited you are about having a business, you will find yourself returning to the workplace or, more adversely, losing everything you have if you don't have a well-thought-out plan. Although my story began in my parents' basement, this is not a path I am recommending to you. However, if you do what I am showing you in this book, you can avoid hitting the same pitfalls and learn from my mistakes.

Let me go a bit deeper into what an escape plan is and what it should include. My plan included how much money I needed to make in order to comfortably provide for the life I wanted. I always wanted to be a millionaire, but in my escape plan, I knew I wouldn't need to have $83,333 per month to live comfortably. In my plan, I listed the lowest amount I needed to earn without sacrificing my family's needs or lifestyle. I included everything in that plan. I wrote out the maximum and the minimum amount of money my family and I needed to meet our budget. With my escape plan, I felt more confident about making such a life-changing decision.

When you are writing out your plan, write the actual number you want to earn. If you want to make a million dollars, write that out. It doesn't matter the number, just be confident that you can have whatever number you believe; anything is possible. Think about a number that you can realistically make because you are willing to put in the work. Now, realistic for you is probably not the same as someone else. Everybody's number is different, so don't ask your friends or family what they feel your number should be. This is your moment of truth. Only you know how much your bills are and the minimum amount you can make in your business to keep your head above water. I am going to challenge you to start thinking of that number and make that your goal. I would suggest you start with the absolute lowest number you think you can do and crush it.

Below are some questions you can include in your escape plan. Remember, the more well thought out your decisions regarding your business, the more benefits you will reap in the long run.

1. When do you want to start full-time in your business?

2. How much time (how many months) will it take you to be financially prepared?

3. What are your annual monetary goals? (Write an actual number here.)

   a. What are your monthly monetary goals?

4. How much money do you need to meet your household budget?

> Millionaire Secret #5- Write out the actual number you want to earn in your business. Writing it down increases your likelihood of reaching your goals.

How did it feel to process through those questions? Are you sensing a bit more clarity and confidence? Well, while your entrepreneur juices are flowing, I want you to keep defining your business. So let's keep defining your business.

Product or Service Based

Now that I have your thoughts churning, let's go a bit further. The next thing for you to decide is if you are going to offer a product or if you are going to provide a service in your business. This is especially important when starting your business. Your website, what you sell, and what you're offering could be a product that you've created. An example of this could be a book, a course, training or workshops, or physical items. A service-based business will include consulting for other businesses, coaching, or assisting with something another company needs, i.e., a virtual assistant, a ghostwriter, etc.

Deciding between a product or service will be really important when you're establishing your business because this will determine the look of your website. With a product-based business, you're going to need an online shopping cart and ways for people to buy your product. If you're selling a service, you're going to need an application process so that you can speak with potential clients who want to work with you to see if you are a good fit. I do both; I sell products and offer services. When you're first starting up a business, you need to stay in one lane.

> Millionaire Secret #6- The true entrepreneur actually does the service or provides the product in most cases before they're paid.

The focus of this book is to help you with the basics of starting your new business, so I want you to reflect on the questions below. Every new business owner will need to answer questions about their new business. These are the preliminary questions and a good foundational start.

1. Identify what type of business you would like to have.
2. What business (industry) is this in?
3. Is this a thriving industry with proven results?

4. What is the name of your business? (Think of a name that makes it easier for a customer to find you, and it clearly exhibits what your company offers.)
5. Is this a product-based or service-based business?
6. Where will your business be located (online, physical location, home office)?

Once you have finalized your business name and determined the type of business you are going to start, you'll move immediately into setting up a professional business profile and online presence. Every true business owner should have a corporation set up. Your business should be handled as a professional business and not a side-hustle. Even if you begin your business part-time, it should never appear like your business is not your focus. Your potential customers will be able to tell if you are a professional, and trust me, this is not an area you want to sacrifice. When a customer doesn't believe you are in a business that you are committed to, they will not spend money with you. On the day of "air out your grievances online," you don't want to get caught with a customer leaving a negative review about your business.

I will not spend a lot of time on what you need to do to set up a professional business because I have a few videos available on my YouTube channel on the subject. I also spoke extensively on this in my free book *Real Estate Millionaire Secrets*. Either of these resources will give you a more in-depth breakdown of how to set up a business.

Grow Your Wealth Blueprint

- Name your Business.
- Get your Domain Name.
- Create a Business Plan. (A Business Plan is required for some business loans.)
- Determine the Budget.
- Analyze your Family Support. (Who is your support system?)
- Select a Business Name. (Conduct a quick "Google" search to ensure the name is not already taken.)
- Purchase a Domain.
- Register your Business with the Secretary of State.
- Apply for an EIN. (www.irs.gov)
- Apply for a DUNS & Bradstreet Number.
- Open a Business Bank Account.
- Set up a Website. (Add a "Coming Soon" landing page until your website is created; make sure to include a sign-up link to start collecting email addresses.)
- Decide on your Brand.

- Create your Social Media Accounts.
- Create a Social Media Marketing Plan.
- Set up your Accounting System & Start Making Money!

Chapter Recap:

- Start the business that you would be willing to work both day and night without any compensation.

- The true entrepreneur does the service or provides the product in most cases before they're paid.

- If you pursue anything just for the income and not the love of the opportunity, you will find yourself bored and frustrated, which will in turn limit you.

- No matter how excited you are about having a business, if you don't have a well-thought-out plan, you will find yourself returning to the workplace or, more adversely, losing everything you have.

- Set up a professional business profile and online presence.

WHAT BUSINESS SUITS YOU?

Notes:

CHAPTER FOUR:
BECOME AN EXPERT IN YOUR INDUSTRY

"Every problem is a gift—without problems, we would not grow."
- Anthony Robbins

I am thankful for the day I learned how to help solve more customers' problems. Mastering this skill afforded me the opportunity to create a system with multiple streams of income. I believe the *Grow Your Wealth Blueprint* can be applied to any business model. Allow me to give you an example of how this worked in my real estate business to help me expand the brand.

When I first started in real estate, I began with wholesaling. After I became really good at wholesaling, I graduated to fixing and flipping houses. From there, I started purchasing rental properties. That led me to expand more. It was then that I discovered a need in the marketplace that wasn't being filled. I realized that HGTV and the other fix and flip shows were not showing people how to truly fix and flip a home. People expressed that they needed real information, and not just some numbers put up on a television screen. They really wanted to see how much it would cost for a project. People wanted to know how to fix and flip with real-world scenarios, contractors, and problems. So I had an idea to start offering tours of my fix and flips and tours of my rental properties to teach and show people what I knew.

This was a need in the marketplace and an area where I could bring a ton of value. People paid me $500 for one day to come on a tour of my properties and for me to educate them on how I did it. As I continued doing this, in one weekend, I was making $10,000, $20,000, and $30,000 just by sharing my knowledge. As I grew my niche and started coaching more students, I began writing books, recording podcasts, and premiering videos on YouTube. Word about my business began to spread, and I was offered opportunities to speak on other people's stages. Speaking engagements created more exposure for me and my business. This is how you can become an expert in your industry.

Become An Expert

So, let me recap what I did and how I started making money as I emerged in the real estate industry. The first thing I did was stick with one industry. I didn't try to build in multiple industries at the same time. Instead, I stayed in the same industry and learned whatever I could to advance myself. So, not only do you need to be passionate about starting a viable business, but you also need to become an expert. When your customers mention your industry, you want them to think of you. When people mention real estate courses and coaches, they mention my name. But, it wasn't always this way. I became known outside of my sphere of influence when I became an expert.

Being successful in business requires that you become a specialist in your field. Think about this in the field of medicine. Doesn't a doctor who is a specialist in a particular area charge more than a general doctor or a public clinic? Now think about this as it relates to your new business. Becoming an expert will help you reach millionaire status in less time than if you stayed as a generalist. First, you start with your one core business. Then you figure out what type of people you want to work with, you find out what problems they are having, and then you solve those problems. This is the strategy for success.

> Millionaire Secret# 7- Every Millionaire is an expert in an industry or niche.

Who is your Ideal Client?

One of the first things you will need to establish in becoming an expert is being clear about the identity of your ideal client. Since I began in real estate full time, I have been able to find steady customers that need what I offer. Because of this, I have been able to cater my services and programs to fit their needs. For example, when I realized that I liked working with people who were behind on their mortgage payments, I began to target those customers to offer my assistance. Because I had also experienced foreclosure, I was passionate about saving others from the downfall I had experienced when I had to return to my parent's basement. I knew how they were feeling; I knew the emotional strain it had on them. I knew the fear and embarrassment that came along with it, and now I knew how to solve it for them. I created value for myself by getting rental properties, and I saved them from going into foreclosure. I had discovered my ideal client, and it was a total win-win situation.

Here are some questions to answer about your ideal client and your solutions for them.

Who are your customers (ideal clients)?

What products or services will you offer them?

Who are the key players in the industry?

What will you offer that will make your business stand out?

How much experience do you have in this area? If you don't have much experience, are you willing to commit to a mentor or teacher in your industry?

> Millionaire Secret #8- One of the first things you will need to establish in becoming an expert is being clear about the identity of your ideal client.

Educate Yourself

Becoming an expert will require you to obtain the necessary education you need to master your industry and then be able to teach and help others. I have been able to help so many people find financial freedom as a result of becoming an expert in real estate. I will probably never know the number of people I have impacted, but I do know it's quite a bit. Therefore, I can attest to my success in becoming an expert.

When I decided that I wanted to become a millionaire in real estate, I started studying all aspects of it. I learned Wholesaling, Subject-Tos, Foreclosures, Pre-Foreclosures. I learned about hard money lenders, business credit, marketing, and team building. Also, I hired a coach, and whatever my coach taught me, I immediately put it into action. I left no stone unturned because I was determined to master this.

You will need to have the same tenacity and drive as you build your business. Take the time to educate yourself about the industry and field you want to enter. Learn who the major players are and take notes from them. Work on your craft and become an expert in whatever you want to do. Can I also suggest that your education be well-rounded? In other words, don't just spend a ton of time watching YouTube videos from various influencers and classify that as education. You must be careful about watching tons of videos with many different people giving you all different types of advice. This is so important. Take your education seriously. You would not go to four different colleges at the same time. You wouldn't take fourteen different classes at a time, right? See your business education the same way.

Solve Your Ideal Clients Problems

Damon John said it best, "In a niche market, you have to find your angle. Ask yourself: What is the competition not doing that is in-demand and I could do well? Then, attack."[2] The business owner who is clear about who they serve and what products they offer that show their level of expertise and adds to their credibility will always win. A mistake that many new business owners make is they try to serve everyone. There is no way possible that everyone from all races and cultures will be attracted to what you have to offer. Even today, I reach a wide array of cultures and income levels, but there are still those that may not relate to me. I am perfectly okay with that, and I don't take it personally when they choose another business or expert over me. You will need to take this same approach when you think about your ideal customers and the problem(s) you will be solving for them.

Before you can solve their problems, you need to spend some time finding out what their problems are. Don't just assume that you know what people need. I didn't just start giving tours of my properties – I began by answering my students' questions. They were seeking real solutions to fixing and flipping, and they came to me because it was my area of expertise.

---

2   Twitter- John, Daymond [@TheSharkDaymond]. [2019, March 3] #SharkTank [Tweet] https://twitter.com/thesharkdaymond/status/1102405061299318785

Research and Implementation

Market research in any business is key. Your research can include targeting people who you know would be an ideal client. It can also involve creating surveys on social media and listening to what people are saying. It could also include researching case studies about your industry. You can do your research in so many ways – the important thing is that you do it. Doing your research will also help you determine how much your ideal client is willing to pay for your services.

Also, let me advise that even more important than doing research is the implementation of the research. Don't get stuck in the paralysis analysis phase where you're just analyzing everything to death, and you're not doing anything. The reason why you research is, so you know the right way for you to go in your business. You should then take action on your business idea.

> Millionaire Secret #9- The business owner who is clear about who they serve and what products they offer that show their level of expertise and adds to their credibility will always win.

"The most influential thought leaders and experts have one thing in common: They never stop learning. Making it to the top doesn't guarantee you will stay there long. As your industry changes, staying one step ahead of trends and developments is imperative for growth."[3]

---

3 Tanya Hall, "How to Become an Industry Expert This Year, The road to thought leadership takes time and dedication, but building your personal brand and audience will pay off in the long run" Inc, January 16, 2020. https://www.inc.com/tanya-hall/how-to-become-an-industry-expert-this-year.html (accessed June 20th, 2021)

Solution, Price, and Packaging:

One of the methods I used when I began my real estate business was a wisdom nugget my coach taught me. He said, "find people that can afford to pay for your services." This concept really hit home to me as I was doing wholesaling at the time. Because my passion was to help people who were struggling, I had to think bigger than their situation to get them the help they needed. After he said this, I started concentrating more on finding the right investors. The investors were ultimately who my business was serving. This one concept allowed me to find investors to help solve people's problems, and in return, I was able to get a nice-sized check.

> Millionaire Secret #10- Find people whose problems you solve, and they have the money to pay you for it.

Be a Solution to People's Problems

I am sure this may be much for you to chew on, so I want you to really take some time to think about this. You are paid according to the size of the problem you solve for others. When I'm helping people that are in foreclosure, they are not my actual customers. Although they benefit from my services, who I am really helping to make a profit is the investors. They are the people who are paying me the $5,000, not the people with the property problems. Does that make sense?

Let me give you another example of how easy it is to create revenue in your business. I've helped many people increase their income. If you don't have the financial capital to fund your business ideas, consider offering your services to the people who can pay you. There are no out-of-cost expenses to run a service-based business during the initial start phases. Have you ever considered professionals like lawyers, doctors, dentists, and chiropractors need help finding clients? Yes, they do! I can almost guarantee that they are so busy with patients during the day they don't have time for sales and marketing. I have many testimonies from people who became rich because they started helping people with money solve their problems. Most people that have a business are looking for more clients. If you can help them find clients, they will pay you. You can go on social media and find many professionals who need help. You can help them make videos, keep up their YouTube page and keep their brand fresh. These are just some ideas to help you generate revenue for your business.

The bigger the problem you solve, the more money you will make.

What problem will your business solve?

What problem will your products or services that you provide in the business solve?

Once you have decided on your business and understand your ideal client market, you will need to decide on your pricing and packaging. First, think about the value you will bring to your customer. Now think about how much they would be willing to pay you for it. If you don't know what to charge, do your research on what customers are paying for the same services that you offer. After finding this, see if you can add additional value and increase the price by 15 - 20% percent. If you want to create a million-dollar business, you will need to have some high-ticket items. Don't be afraid to charge your worth.

I recently had a conversation with a videographer about how he could add additional value to his customers while increasing his annual profit. He didn't know how to create this, so I gave him an idea. I said, "why don't you package your services, and instead of charging for one session of $150, you can charge $100 a month, and your clients get a session each month?" He hadn't thought of that. But, with just a minor tweak, he offered a product that his clients would be willing to pay him monthly and not just collect a one-time fee.

Put some thought into how you can make a model like this work in your business.

Chapter Recap

- Not only do you need to be passionate about starting a viable business – but you also need to become an expert.
- Take the time to educate yourself about the industry and field you want to enter.
- Don't get stuck in the paralysis analysis phase where you're just analyzing everything to death, and you're not doing anything. The reason you research is, so you know the right way for you to go in your business.
- The bigger the problem you solve, the more money you will make.
- Think about the value you will bring to your customer. Now think about how much they would be willing to pay you for it.

Notes:

CHAPTER FIVE:
WHERE ARE YOUR CUSTOMERS?

"The first step is to establish that something is possible, then probability will occur."
- Elon Musk

The Secret Sauce to finding your customers is to give first. But I don't want to get ahead of myself, so before I jump into that, I want to offer you a bit of motivation. There are billions of people in this world, and the internet has made it possible for you to connect with many customers at any time, thus creating unlimited access to customers ready to buy your service or products. Of course, as with anything, there are pros and cons. The pro is that you have access to many people ready to spend money with you. The con is that sometimes even the best marketing and sales strategies won't keep some of the "not so ideal" customers away.

There is a way to advertise and market your business where you only attract your ideal customers. You don't have to be afraid that you will have to work for people you don't like who will drive you crazy just because you need the money. Not only does being an entrepreneur give you freedom, but it gives you the freedom to choose. Having a business and being an entrepreneur is like being an employee because you get to pick and choose who you work with. You have your choice of companies, and just the same, you don't have to work with any customer or client that comes into your business.

Now that we've cleared that up let's explore how to find the customers you want to work with. The "Give-First" model is one that I have incorporated and have had major success in finding my ideal client. Let me explain it to you. When I started in my real estate business, one of the things that I did was find additional ways to help people with their real estate problems. For example, instead of just asking them if they were behind in their mortgage, I started educating them for free on how to avoid foreclosures and let them know what happens during the foreclosure process. I helped people through the modification process, and I helped them learn how they could sell their homes without a realtor. I started presenting different ways to help them.

I created a free report online that listed seven ways to sell a house without a realtor with this valuable information. Now think about how helpful this was to someone facing a foreclosure. This was priceless to the people who were behind on their mortgage payments and needed to do repairs, and didn't have a lot of equity in the home, so hiring a realtor to sell their home was not the best option. I gave them the tips absolutely free. In return, they gave me their email in exchange for the report.

This is how I was able to start pulling in customers that I wanted to work with. Many of them would call and ask for more information or tell me they enjoyed the checklist. Before long, I had a database of people that I could choose from. This is how you acquire a pick of your ideal clients. Give first!

Using that example, think about what you can incorporate into your business to give away to your ideal customer for free. Some ideas for freebies include newsletters, hosting events & seminars, and speaking engagements. As clever as I am, I wasn't the first to come up with this model. In the malls in Florida, the restaurants in the food courts are always giving out samples to hungry buyers walking by their booth. Do you know how many people buy from the food stations just because they had a sample? The person could have been heading to another restaurant, but they were hooked once they tasted a savory bite. The big-box retailer Costco is another example of this. I am guilty of going to their store to purchase one food item, but I added something that wasn't on my list to my shopping cart because of a sample taste. This model works!

> Millionaire Secrets # 11- The Give-First Model is how you create major success in finding your ideal client.

After you have successfully incorporated this strategy, think about how you will turn your interested audience into actual clients. What I like about the model is that it triggers the Law of Reciprocity. You will find that people often want to give back when they receive something. Have you ever noticed that some people don't like accepting something for free? If they do, they feel like they owe you. Well, this is a good thing in business. You want people to feel like you've brought them value and that they owe you in some way. From there, you can start making offers. You've given your audience something of value for free, you've triggered the Law of Reciprocity, and now you can make an offer to them in that order.

> Millionaire Secret #12- The Give-First Model triggers the Law of Reciprocity.

Your Freebie

Be selective about your customers and be strategic with your freebie. Think about who you target. Who is the ideal client that you want to pull in? What problems of theirs can you address in your freebie? Then, be very deliberate and make your offer around what your ideal customer would want. Let me repeat that. Make your offer around what your ideal customer would want.

Find More Customers

Additionally, you want to market your business both online and offline. I don't care if you're just an online business – you should be marketing offline as well. You should have letters, billboards, flyers, or other marketing materials that you can hand out physically to tell people about your business. If you have a physical business or a brick and mortar, you should include online marketing. Every business owner should be marketing their business both online and offline. That is the key to getting more customers. Do not focus on just one or the other; you must do both. It's super easy, and in many cases, it's absolutely free.

Chapter Recap

- The Secret Sauce to finding your customers is to give first.
- The Gift-First Model will help you attract your ideal client.
- Some suggestions for freebies include newsletters, hosting events & seminars, and speaking engagements.
- Market your business both online and offline to reach more customers.

WHERE ARE YOUR CUSTOMERS?

Notes:

CHAPTER SIX:
LEARN, DO & TEACH

"Success is not final; failure is not fatal: it is the courage to continue that counts."
- Winston Churchill

Operating a new business can seem overwhelming, especially when dealing with irate customers, difficult team members, late-paying vendors, and the list can go on from there. Rest assured that the good days will outweigh the bad days. If you wake up with the determination to win every day, you will succeed. Many new entrepreneurs want to throw in the towel when they don't see quick results, and they get frustrated during the building stages of their business. They can often be sidetracked by the portrayals of success on social media, or they get discouraged when they think others are making money and they're not.

The envy of a thriving business is comparison. This is a good topic for us to address because many entrepreneurs look at millionaire business owners or successful people and want to be on the same income earning level during their first few years of business. You should never compare your business and life to what you see others accomplishing. Many new entrepreneurs get caught into the trap of comparing their lives to others, hoping and wishing they had the things others had. It's almost as if they believe that instead of starting from the ground up, they can magically skip the necessary steps or cheat their way to the top. You can't – none of us could.

I always advise my students to keep their eyes focused on where they are instead of looking at what someone else is doing. You can never win a race looking back at the other runners. Keep this in mind. I want you to keep your consistent focus on what you do and build a business that serves others. Once you build a business that can serve more people, you will never experience lack. This is the type of business that will always give back to you time and time again. It's the law of sowing and reaping at work. What you sow is what you will receive in even more abundance.

The most successful entrepreneurs know that building a business empire is less about just serving your needs but helping more people get what they need. In the process, as you are serving others, your dreams will also manifest. I can't tell you how or why it happens that way – I can just say that it does. Trust me!

Of course, this doesn't mean that you neglect yourself and what you desire in this life. Oh no, I want you to dream big! I want you to build your dream the way you see it and the way that best suits you. In other words, the business journey you are on is about you receiving the financial legacy you deserve!

> Millionaire Secret #13- The most successful entrepreneurs are those that know building a business empire is less about just serving your needs but helping more people get what they need.

Coaching and Mentoring

One way of serving people in your business is by coaching and mentoring others. Many people want a coach or a mentor so that they can fast track their way to success. They don't want to hire a coach or a mentor and still struggle with the same issues that someone without a coach will struggle with. They want to be able to transform where they are and have a clear path and plan on how to reach their goals. This can be in any area in which you have a lot of knowledge and experience. Photography, cooking, book writing, real estate, parenting, event planning – the list is endless. I have met many different coaches: life coaches, fitness coaches, lifestyle coaches, and nutrition coaches, each offering their clients a clear transformation in their area of expertise.

After you master your skills, think about how you can help others in their life journey. It's about each of us playing our part in the world or paying it forward. I find coaching and mentoring people to be one of the most fulfilling things in my life and my business. You literally can create a program that works for you and provide real results for others, and it is beneficial for both you and the student. It also creates an additional stream of revenue for your business.

If you have never coached and mentored before, it may seem intimidating at first but trust me – you can do it. Coaching is simply creating a program or service that helps your student reach a desired goal quicker than if they tried to attempt it on their own. If you know how to do something well, you can probably explain it to others. Quite honestly, you are probably already doing this and not even noticing that you are doing so. Let me explain what I mean. If a friend calls you for advice in a particular area and you give them advice on what they should do and helps them, you have offered them coaching. If you package that advice with clear action steps, anticipated goals, a desired outcome, and some accompanying worksheets, you have already assembled your first coaching program. It's a lot easier than you think.

When you think about coaching others, the first thing that you need to write down is what transformation you can offer. Think about the areas in your life that you can help others in where you have been successful. This can be a personal success, spiritual, business, or any area where you have achieved a measure of success. People need coaching in everything. Next, think about any area you have been successful at that you are passionate about and willing to teach. Finally, think about the system you used to get there. Did you have a coach? Did you study a particular subject? Did you take a class or seminar? Did you make any mental adjustments? Did you learn any new habits? Did you implement any new daily activities? All of these things are components of your transformation system.

Now think about the mistakes that you have made. Think about the pitfalls and obstacles. Think about your learning experiences and what you can help others avoid. These are also essential components to helping others find success. In fact, that's probably going to be the most valuable thing in your coaching program. Listing the different things you've attempted and the different mistakes you've made will help save your participants time and money, and who wouldn't want to save both of those?

When I started mentoring, I used my story to connect with my students. I had to first be successful in quitting the job and transitioned to become an entrepreneur in real estate in order to teach them how to. I shared with the students exactly what I did; I shared my failures as well as my wins. You don't really want to just transform people in one area – you want to give them your entire story. So, what is it that you have changed about yourself? Now think about how you can provide that same step-by-step process for someone else to follow.

Here are some questions you can answer to help you scope out your program.

What transformation can you help someone achieve?

How long have you had success in this area?

What are the key points to finding success in this area?

What personal stories can you tell to help show your own transformation?

Who would benefit from your transformation (your ideal client)?

What are some of the tools that you use?

What are some of the resources, websites?

What are some things you did wrong that you would tell them to avoid and tell them why?

Creating Your Program

The next thing you want to do is take the transformation you offer and break that down into a program or a course. Use real-life experiences to add validity to your program. Your potential clients will want to see the transformation others have had. Make sure you are honest and don't make up stories or content that is not true. If you haven't been able to assemble actual testimonies and case studies, start finding people who need the transformation you offer and offer them your services for free or at a minimum cost. This would be your pilot program.

To create the program, think about your ideal client. Your ideal client is someone like you, who is in a similar position to where you used to be before becoming successful. As you build your coaching program, write down the process of reaching the desired results. The steps that you took are what you'll use to create the teaching segments and coaching modules. Accompany this content with videos that clearly state the actions that your ideal client needs to take to reach the desired outcome throughout the videos and coursework. Let me give you an example of this. I have students that want to learn real estate and immediately want to jump into fixing and flipping. In my programs, I warn them of the dangers of how this backfired on me and how it landed me in my parent's basement. I tell them that just because a hard money lender will loan you the money to fix and flip a house doesn't mean that's what you should be doing. I instead teach them things I have learned and offer them the right way to approach real estate as a newbie. The information in my program helps guide them on how to avoid real estate pitfalls.

Your students will ultimately want to know what you did and how you did it.

Once you've created your signature program or course, go and find your tribe. Also, let me add this nugget for you. You cannot coach or mentor everyone; sometimes, some people just are not a good fit. I'm particular about the type of people that I can work with. It's not just about if they have the money to pay for my course or my program, but if they also match with the culture of my business.

In fact, I have thousands and thousands of subscribers and people that contact me regularly, but I work with less than 1% of all the people that ever contact me because they're not a fit for my business. So, regardless of whether they have the money or the time, I want to make sure that they will be a good fit and find the success they need.

When you first start, think of a niche client. For example, when I first started, I worked with women. These women were moms, women like me, and women who have worked in Corporate America. These were people that I could relate to, and I knew how to help them best. Now that I've grown and my company is much bigger with more employees, I can take on different types of clients, as long as they have the basic skills, knowledge, and acumen to be successful in the program.

In the beginning, you may start with just a small group of people – maybe, only five people. I literally was able to make six figures working with just five or six people at a time. I now can make over seven figures in my coaching business because I can work with more students, and I can charge a higher premium because I've learned more things.

> Millionaire Secret #14- To create the program, think about your ideal client. Your ideal client is someone like you, who is in a similar position to where you used to be before you became successful.

As you build a business that serves, I want you to keep some additional things in mind. First, you must set clear boundaries in your business. Being in service to others does not mean you allow clients to run over you and set the rules in your business. You are the owner and ultimately responsible for your business. Some of the key areas to establish boundaries in are:

- Establishing hours of operations.
- Standard operating procedures.
- Client relation management systems.
- Clearly define the scope of your services.
- Clearly define your pricing structure.

Many entrepreneurs believe that being in service to others means they will need to be people pleasers. Remember that every client won't be a good fit for you, and that's okay. As you become more experienced in business, you feel more comfortable in setting established boundaries.

Chapter Recap

- One way of serving people in your business is by coaching and mentoring others.

- Coaching is simply creating a program or service that helps your student reach a desired goal quicker than if they tried to attempt it on their own.

- When you think about coaching others, the first thing that you need to write down is what transformation you can offer.

- As you build your coaching program, write down the process of reaching the desired results. The steps that you took are what you'll use to create the teaching segments and coaching modules.

- You must set clear boundaries in your business. Being in service to others does not mean you allow clients to run over you and set the rules in your business.

Notes:

CHAPTER SEVEN:
GROWING A MILLION DOLLAR BRAND

"Focus on your strengths, not your weaknesses. Focus on your character, not your reputation. Focus on your blessings, not your misfortunes."
- Roy T. Bennett

Communication is probably the most important skill that you will need to develop as a millionaire and grow a million-dollar brand. Communication includes being able to speak well. However, more than speaking well, good communication also includes expressing your ideas and thoughts clearly. Every millionaire that I know has the great skill of being able to communicate effectively. If you are weak in your communication skills, you should focus on improving them. Learning to communicate effectively was a game-changer for me in my business. It was such an essential skill for me to master that I hired coaches to help me. I have had coaches who helped me on camera and coaches who trained me to speak on stage. Communication is key – you must learn how to master it.

> Millionaire Secret #15- Every millionaire that I know has the great skill of being able to communicate effectively.

Influence

Being able to influence other people is a skill that you need to develop. As a real estate entrepreneur, I did not understand how important it was to be able to influence others. I had been a manager in Corporate America who was able to dictate to others what to do. As the manager, I was used to authority that was given to me by upper management. I quickly realized that running a business is different. Although you are a manager in your business, if you can't influence people to hire you, work with you, or buy your products, you won't be in business for very long. Having authority and having influence are two different things.

Over the years, I transitioned from thousand dollars influence to million dollars influence. It required growth to do so. Influence gets people to do things without telling them to do it. To get people to subscribe to your website, buy your products and services, buy your books without you having to ask them or beg them is the true test of your influence. Have you ever heard of the saying, 'people do business with people they like?' Being likable and relatable are important and are tied to your level of influence.

Being able to influence someone does not mean you have any authority over them. You don't have to be a manager or the United States president or have any titles to influence a person. To be a person of influence, you need to know how to influence people. To learn how to do this, start with a book by John Maxwell, which I read called *Becoming A Person Of Influence*. It was life-changing for me.

> Millionaire Secret #16- If you can't influence people to hire you, work with you, or buy your products, you won't be in business for very long.

Marketing

Marketing! Marketing! Marketing! If you say you want to be a millionaire, you will have to get good at marketing. Unfortunately, I was not good at marketing when I started my business. I did not know how to market myself, and I did not know how to market my business. It was a skill that I really had to develop. And it is a skill that has taken me years to grasp; in fact, I'm still learning how to do this today.

How do you sell yourself? How do you sell your products and your services? You have to work on this skill. You cannot be afraid to market your business. There's no business making millions of dollars that is not well-known; someone has to know. Your customer, most importantly, needs to know about you. So you must market to build a million-dollar brand.

> Millionaire Secret #17- Having authority and having influence are two different things.

An Online Presence

There was a time when I underestimated the value of a social media account. I had an old-school methodology of how to get customers and grow my business, and I really wasn't interested in social media. I know that's hard to believe, but it's true. As a result, I had no idea that real customers were waiting to find me, and I was providing a disservice by not making myself available online. Let's just say now that I know better, and I will never make that mistake again.

Establishing an online presence is not about a popularity contest. It's not about how many likes and shares you will get; It is so much bigger than that. It's about connecting with your audience, and the best way to do that is to add value. Besides, social media is a free and easy way to grow and let your customers know that you are in business. Although I slept on this free billboard, I want to make sure you start off on the right foot in your business. If you have not done so already, set up a social media business page for your business. You should use all the major social media accounts: Facebook, Instagram, Twitter, LinkedIn. I would even suggest adding TikTok or any other social media where your customers are spending their time.

I can almost hear your rebuttal to this. It's not uncommon for new business owners to shy away from social media because they don't want to tell their friends and family that they have a business. After all, they want to keep the nosey people and the haters out. I understand how you feel; however, that doesn't change the fact that you must be willing to establish your online presence. You will have to silence the doubters and the nosey people because they will cost you hundreds, thousands, and even millions of dollars. Is it worth it? Hiding your business is giving them unnecessary power, and ultimately they are silencing your voice. I am sure you don't want that. Go on to social media and tell your audience what you do, what customers you serve, and how you serve them. Don't be ashamed to let them know you are looking for customers. I am sure that people will be reaching out to you soon. Let me leave one of my favorite quotes here with you, "ask, and you shall receive."

Sales

Sales are an important skill for every millionaire, so this is something you are going to have to develop. Having sales in your business is your life support. Most people have no idea how to sell anything. They are uncomfortable selling, and they don't like the idea of selling. Sales go hand in hand with marketing. Marketing and sales are not the same thing, but they are very intertwined.

You have to be able to advertise and market your products to people. Then, when you get them on the phone, in your store, or in your office, you need to be able to convert them. If you are not good at selling or not something you enjoy, you're probably never going to be a millionaire. I'm just being honest with you. Almost every millionaire that I know, no matter their personality, is a master at selling. Even the people who don't even like talking a lot know how to sell their products and services.

It doesn't matter if you can sell everything. You don't have to be the person who can sell ice to an Eskimo, but you need to sell your product and your service very well if you want to be a millionaire.

> Millionaire Secret #18- Almost every millionaire, no matter their personality, is a master at selling.

Planning

Planning seems to be the easiest layer as most people are pretty good at it. And I can honestly say this is not something that a lot of people struggle with. Millionaires are really good at planning and organizing their day, week, month, and year. Thankfully, this was not a struggle for me; I was pretty good at planning. I can easily write down a plan with the steps on how to create it. The major difference between the old me and the millionaire-me is I know how to execute a plan. That is where most people fall in business. Many people can write down a plan, write down what they're going to do, and write down their goals. That's the easy part. The more complicated part is executing the plan. To become a millionaire, not only do you make a plan, but you must execute your plan. Therefore, you need to develop the skill to do both of those things.

Chapter Recap

- Communication is probably the most important skill that you will need to develop as a millionaire.

- Being able to influence other people is a skill that you need to develop. However, being able to influence someone does not mean you have any authority over them.

- Sales are an important skill for any millionaire. This is something you are going to have to develop.

- To become a millionaire, not only do you make a plan, but you must execute your plan.

Notes:

CHAPTER EIGHT:
GET YOUR BUSINESS FUNDED

Business is other people's money.
- Author: Delphine De Girardin

One of the biggest pitfalls that most business owners encounter is a lack of funding. Their income fluctuates from month to month, therefore making it difficult to grow their business. One month they're making money, and then the next month, the income is down. This isn't abnormal because there will always be some income months that are higher than others when you are operating a business. Weathering that storm of uncertainty can create a lot of anxiety for people pushing them to want to quit and give up. I think there is an easier way to overcome this, and that is with business funding. Many business owners have been ignorant about how much funding is available for businesses once a business is set up correctly. Even more surprising is that it does not have anything to do with your personal credit, and your business doesn't even need to be making much income for them to loan you funding for your business.

There's so much to business credit that really helps a business owner, but unfortunately, many business owners are not knowledgeable about how it works. I had my business for so many years before I ever learned about business credit and business funding. Trying to fund your business through personal credit or your personal savings can limit your business expansion. So maybe you're wondering, okay, this sounds great, I'm interested, where do I begin? The first thing that everyone has to do is start the business on paper. We've already talked about going from idea to inception but allow me to give you a quick recap.

No matter what business you decide to start, you need to determine if you are selling a product, a service, or both. Secondly, you need to write out the idea, then make a business plan with precisely what your business will entail. You'll need to have this spelled out thoroughly to receive any business funding. Now don't get too carried away with the business plan. I'm not saying that you need to spend a lot of money to have this professionally done or have someone write up anything for you, but you must get clear on your vision. It is extremely easy to write out a business plan; it doesn't take very long at all. In fact, I have students that have completed a good business plan in an hour or two. It's very good to have a business plan completed before you start your business because you have it available, and it won't seem like you just made it up to get funding.

In the plan, you need to describe:

What does the business do?

Where are the customers coming from?

What do you project the income will be?

Your operating and expense budget.

Once you are clear on the business idea, make sure that you write it out in a way that makes sense. Make sure anyone who reviews it can clearly understand what you do, who your customers are, and how you will make profits. This is the step that most people skip and why most businesses never get off the ground.

> Millionaire Secret #19- Most businesses don't list who their customers are and how they will make a profit in their business plan. This is why they don't get funded.

If you haven't done so already, the next step is to make the business a real business. In other words, set the official business up the right way. Have your business registered with the Secretary of State with a LLC or a C Corp or S Corp. Make it a legal entity, get an EIN, a professional phone number, and get a professional website.

You will need to have these things in place as proof that you have an actual business when they check out your profile. If the credit company or funder searches for you on Google and finds that you have a legitimate business, this will set you apart from most business owners. Once you create your solid profit, people will lend money to you. You'll be surprised at how much money people will lend to your business just for having a decent website, a professional phone number (not your cell phone), and a professional email.

But the key is you need to do these steps so that the business is a legal entity, something that people can actually fund, and something that people can invest in so you can build credit quickly. So, I encourage you to move quickly because I know the significant impact this will have on your business and your profit. Business credit is what changed my business forever. I used to have to use my credit cards and my savings in order to have capital and savings for my business. And I was fine doing that, but it wasn't until I started getting business credit, business lines of credit, credit cards, and all of these funds in my business's name that I was truly able to quit my job and never have to return.

You can do the exact same thing. You can build business credit really quickly if you do the steps that I outlined. But you'll also need to make sure that you get an EIN (Employer Identification Number) and a business checking account and start building business credit with a Dun and Bradstreet number.

There are three business bureaus that you should learn about: Dun and Bradstreet, Equifax Business, and Experian Business. Dun and Bradstreet is the biggest business credit agency, and it is where you want to make sure that you have a business credit profile. Some people will tell you that you can skip this step, but I'll be very honest, I could not get into the millions without having a Dun and Bradstreet credit profile, and fortunately, it's pretty easy to do. I don't know why anyone would tell you to skip this step when it is completely free to get your Duns number. Once you do this, you can start having tradelines on your business profile in just a matter of months.

Once you get your profiles established, you should begin applying for vendor credit. I suggest you start with U.S. companies like Uline, Quill, and Granger, and from there, you can quickly upgrade to securing store business credit cards such as Wal-Mart, gas cards like Chevron and Shell. Next, you can move on to getting credit cards from Citi Business, Chase Business, Capital One, American Express business, and a slew of other lines of credit. Today, I have millions of dollars in my business's name just by doing this process for my businesses and then repeating it over and over with each new business idea that I get. And this is how you can take those business ideas and turn them into cash. So once you started building your business credit, go ahead and apply for help. Do not be afraid to apply for business credit cards, and do not be afraid to apply for funding in your business's name.

Most businesses fail because they do not have enough capital to sustain them. As you know, I used to work full time, and I was a working mom. I used to be the mom that was late picking up my kids from daycare. I was always working overtime if I needed more money. And now I live the life that I love because I have a well-funded business. But, that could not happen if I did not take the time, take a step, take a risk, and apply for business credit. Lastly, I want to leave this gem with you. If you want to build business credit quickly, purchase liquid assets like a car or home in your business name using your business EIN. Don't be afraid to go big.

Chapter Recap

- There's so much to business credit that really helps a business owner, but unfortunately, many business owners are not knowledgeable about how it works.

- It's actually very good to have a business plan completed before you start your business because you have it available, and it won't seem like you just made it up to get funding.

- In the Business Plan, you need to list:
  - What does the business do?
  - Where are the customers coming from?
  - What do you project the income will be?
  - Your operating and expense budget.

- If the credit company or funder searches for you on Google and finds that you have a legitimate business, this will set you apart from most business owners.

- There are three business bureaus that you want to start to learn about. The first one is Dun and Bradstreet, the second one is Equifax Business, and the third is Experian Business.

Notes:

CHAPTER NINE:
THE MILLIONAIRE MINDSET

"I got my start by giving myself a start"
- Madam C.J. Walker, Millionaire

Millionaires have different mindsets. With that renewed mindset comes the forming of healthy habits and character traits that become the foundation to attaining millionaire status. I want to share ten of the practices that I have incorporated in my personal and business life that I believe shifted me to millionaire status. There are more, but let's start with these ten to help you move in the right direction. Some of these practices may be familiar to you but remember, the difference between a millionaire and a non-millionaire is what they put into action. After you go through this list, check off the ones you still need to improve on.

> A new survey has found that there are 13.61 million households that have a net worth of $1 million or more, not including the value of their primary residence. That's more than 10% of households in the US.[4]

On your journey to becoming a millionaire, I want you to start assessing your habits and character traits. Many people overlook these areas because habits can be so subtle that sometimes you may not even realize that you're doing them. It's the small undetectable bad habits that are detrimental to our success. This is your opportunity to have your man or woman in the mirror moment. As you switch from working full-time to becoming a full-time entrepreneur, you will need to change some of your habits. Your mindset will also need to elevate. Remember the vision you envisioned

---

4   Darina Lynkova, 28 Millionaire Statistics: What Percentage of Americans Are Millionaires?", SpendMeNot, updated July 12, 2021. https://spendmenot.com/blog/what-percentage-of-americans-are-millionaires/ (accessed July 12, 2021)

in chapter one. Keep that in front of you as a reminder of what you are working to accomplish.

1. **Affirmations**

I believe affirmations are essential as they ignite a reprogramming in our minds. We have been programmed since we were babies. People have told us negative things about who we are, and we have actually believed some of those things. Now that you have decided to succeed in your life and step out into your own business, you will need to reprogram yourself. It's time for you to tell yourself how you see yourself and what you want to be. You may start by declaring that you are a millionaire before becoming one. You should daily affirm, " I am a success," "I am happy," or "I am great." Whatever "I am" affirmations you say to yourself, I promise you that you will become it – you just need to reprogram yourself.

When I began saying my affirmations, I did not have a million dollars in the bank or have a million dollars in properties. Creating this mindset of a millionaire worked like magic. After a short time, I was doing things that millionaires did. I went to places they went, and I put myself in the right environment. I also sought out the right mentors, and I cleared myself of all of the negative programming. I can gladly admit that it was all worth it.

2. **Journaling**

Another secret of mine I want to share with you is journaling. Incorporating daily journaling was a life changer for me and one of the routines I still do today. I want to let you in on a secret as you may not know this, but only successful people journal. As you are reaching new heights, you will want to write it down. If you want to do something significant and great – write it down. This is a method I use to manifest the life I have. In my journal, I write down all the things that are happening to me; I write down my mood. I write down all of the things that I am grateful for, and I write how I love my life and how things are going for me. I start my day by incorporating my gratitude list. I don't focus on the negative things; I keep my mind focused on the positive. Journaling is very important on your road to millions.

> Millionaire Secret #20- Successful people journal.

3. Emotional Intelligence

I cannot tell you how important it is to have emotional intelligence (EQ). Like how some of us have an IQ or intelligence quotient, we also need an emotional quotient. Emotional intelligence is most often defined as the ability to perceive, use, understand and manage emotions (Wikipedia). In other words, how well do you deal with adversity? How well do you deal with anger? How well do you deal with sadness or depression or when things don't work out for you? It is so important that you have emotional intelligence. You don't want to be a person that just flies off the handle, starts crying, or goes crazy when something happens.

If you are saying you want to be a millionaire, understand that it is a journey. If you're self-made like I am, please know that you will need to have a lot of emotional intelligence. There are going to be people that say hurtful things to you. In this world, you may encounter people that will say racist things or sexist things. People aren't always going to be nice or fair. They may say some of the most disrespectful, crazy things to you, and you will need to have enough emotional intelligence to be able to say "thank you" and walk away without losing your cool, without ruining the deal, without fighting anyone, or anything that may cause you to look immature. Emotional intelligence is one of the skills you must develop if you want to be a millionaire. To increase your emotional intelligence, start training yourself on how to respond instead of reacting to conflict, work on your active listening skills and maintain a positive attitude.

4. **Money Management**

Money management is not a skill that most people have, but I assure you, every millionaire has excellent money management skills. There's no way someone will have a million dollars in cash or assets or earn a million dollars that keep growing year after year without good money management.

If you know that you are not good at money management, I suggest hiring someone who can help teach you how to manage your money. Money management is a skill that you are going to have to develop and master. You can't be afraid to have conversations about money. You can't be afraid to ask people for money for your business. You can't be scared to raise your prices. You have to get good with money and managing your money. It has to be a conversation that you're comfortable with.

As a millionaire, I love talking about money, and I have no problems telling you that I'm a millionaire, and the people I speak to talk the same way back to me. So talking about money and money management is a skill for a millionaire.

There are so many benefits to becoming a millionaire and having all of the money that you need. There are many benefits to earning a very high income. It is so much better than living paycheck to paycheck, worrying about money, or even trying to cut back to save money. I know that many people you listen to on YouTube, on Podcasts and subscribe to on social media will tell you that you really need to cut back if you want to get out of your financial trap. They say things like – you probably need to stop eating out at restaurants and start taking your lunch to work and eat in the break room out of a Tupperware so that you can have some money. But, unfortunately, just cutting back is probably not going to get you rich. I'll be really honest with you – you cannot save your way to being rich. Most people that have millions of dollars did not just save that money. If you want to have a $50 million business or buy a $50 million apartment complex, you're not going to save $50 million.

You have to decide that you no longer want to be trapped and that you no longer want to be held down by a job or by financial distress. You have to make a decision and say to yourself, "I want to make a change, I want to be different, and I no longer want to struggle with money." That is the first step.

Now that I am rich, my life has completely changed. I get to own my own time, and I get to spend time with my kids. I get to go on vacation anywhere I want to go. It is so amazing to have more money than you can even spend, and that is why I'm sharing this information with you.

> Millionaire Secret #21- Millionaires have great money management skills.

5. Taking Risks

Every millionaire takes risks, and if you want to be a millionaire, you have to get very comfortable taking risks as well. This was an area that I struggled with at first. I mentioned earlier that I had constant panic attacks when I was trying to do different things in real estate. I was experiencing thoughts of fear and uncertainty concerning money and the new direction that I was taking. So I had to get more comfortable taking risks because every time something comes along, there will be a risk associated with it. And if you want to be a millionaire, please believe you will have to be a risk-taker.

Now, I'm not talking about being crazy, jumping out of airplanes, and running in front of buses or anything like that. But there is definitely a risk to everything. And so let me be clear, you are not leaving this earth alive, okay? There is a risk to life; none of us is getting out of this thing alive. So know that you will have to take risks as a millionaire – you are not going to die.

In most cases, if you start a business, quit your job, buy a house or invest in a stock, most likely, even if it doesn't work out, you're going to be okay. That is one of the things that I've learned from being around millionaires, billionaires, and successful people; they all know this, and they're very comfortable taking risks.

6. Independent Thinking

Being a millionaire means that you need to learn to be an independent thinker. You should be able to come up with your own thoughts, your own ideas, and your own opinions. You should not be afraid to be different from other people, and you have your own way of thinking. Independent thinking means that you do not just do everything that other people are doing. It's not that you're a contrarian that just goes against what the public is doing or goes against what the masses are doing, but in many instances, you are. The bottom line is, if you want to be a millionaire and start to live a life that is different from most people, you're probably going to think differently than most people.

I want to help prepare you to become a successful business owner. To do so, you will need to take risks and be an independent thinker. So don't be surprised that your thoughts are different from others and that most people are not going to agree and come along with the ideas you have. That's important.

> Millionaire Secret #22- To increase your emotional intelligence, start training yourself on how to respond instead of reacting to conflict, work on your active listening skills and maintain a positive attitude.

7. Have Multiple Streams of Income

A major money trap for people is *only having one stream of income*. Let me say that again, a major trap that keeps people poor is when they have only one stream of income. All of my millionaire and multi-millionaire friends have multiple streams of income. They have money coming in from different places, different sources, at different times, and from different ventures. They don't have all of their eggs in one basket.

Having only one source of income is very stressful, and what would you do if you lost that source of income? Trust me, you don't want to rely on one source of income. So even if you have one source right now, you should be working on creating another source of income. Then when you have that second source, go and create another source. I know this sounds difficult, but it's not. If you can create one source of income, you can create two and build from there.

> Millionaire Secret #23- Millionaires have multiple streams of income.

8. Buy Assets and Stop Buying Junk

Read this out loud, **"I will stop wasting money on things that I do not need."** Stop buying things that have no real purpose. Spending without a plan leads to wasting unnecessary money. Think about the amount of time you have purchased something, although you didn't really need it. You go to the store and buy a brush even though you have a brush already. You buy shampoo when you already have shampoo. You buy hats when you already have twelve hats at home. I'm definitely not saying don't buy anything you need. I buy things; I just don't buy things that have no value. I just don't run into Walmart and Dollar Tree and all of these stores and buy cheap, worthless stuff, bring it to my house and fill up storage units full of it.

I know so many people that go into Walmart, and they'll spend $200 just buying stuff. They buy cheap things that have absolutely no value. Let me repeat it – buying stuff that has no value is worthless. Millionaires buy assets. I buy things that I can make money off of. That is the actual difference between what poor people do versus what rich people do.

If you're going to buy things, make sure it brings you value and possibly something that has value that you could sell later. If what you buy represents your business, like clothes or hats and things like that, let it serve a purpose. You put on your business name and your logo, and you advertise your business. But don't just go to Walmart (I'm sorry, Walmart) and buy a bunch of crap every week and wonder why you don't have any money. You need to stop doing that and start spending your money in better places. In other words, you need to stop spending your money and start investing it.

> Millionaire Secret #24- Millionaires don't buy junk; they buy assets.

9. Invest in Yourself

Rich people invest in themselves. One of the money traps that people have is not investing in themselves. Millionaires spend tons of money investing in themselves. They buy educational courses, attend seminars, buy books, hire coaches, hire personal trainers, and anything necessary to better themselves. You are your biggest investment; invest in yourself so that you can be more valuable to the marketplace.

Start bettering yourself, and do not hesitate to spend money investing in yourself. So many people told me that I was absolutely crazy when I was in my parents' basement, bankrupt, broke, with multiple foreclosures and bad credit, and I hired a real estate coach. Boy, were they wrong. That was one of the smartest decisions that I ever made. I realized that I needed to learn something; I needed to understand what I was doing. I needed to learn what my coach knew so that I could build a successful and profitable real estate portfolio. It is so important that you start investing in yourself and learning the skills you need to be successful and make more money. I am proof that this works.

10. **Personal Development**

Whatever you do, always make personal development a priority. I know that sounds "airy-fairy," but if you are struggling in your business, stop focusing on the business and start working on your inner self. Did you know that your business is a reflection of you 100%? Yes, that's right! If your business makes $50,000 a year, it's because that's what you think it's worth. If your business is making $100,000 a year or $200,000, whatever it's making or not making is because of you as the owner. So if you want it to do more and you want the struggle to end, you're going to have to look inside yourself. You're going to need to start seeing worthiness, start being deserving, and start doing the things that you want to do. So often, we do things in our business that we don't even enjoy doing. Stop doing those things. Only do the things that you want to do, and you will actually make more money. Trust me on this; I struggled with those thoughts and ideas. I just did not think that it was possible, and now, I really do. I operate in my business in a way that makes me really happy, and I am making more money than I've ever made.

Learn the tools and experience NOELLE RANDALL live or virtual at www.NoelleRandallEvents.com. Use code "BMS" to save 50% on tickets

Chapter Recap

- As you switch from working full-time to becoming a full-time entrepreneur, you will need to change some of your habits. Your mindset will also need to elevate.
- Affirmations are essential as they ignite a reprogramming in our minds.
- Emotional intelligence is one of the skills you must develop if you want to be a millionaire. To increase your emotional intelligence, start training yourself on how to respond instead of reacting to conflict, work on your active listening skills and maintain a positive attitude.
- Millionaires have multiple streams of income.
- Whatever you do, always make personal development a priority.

Notes:

CHAPTER TEN:
TO YOUR SUCCESS

"It always seems impossible until it's done."
  - Nelson Mandela

Before we end this book, I want to introduce you to one of my student success stories. I like to highlight my students on my YouTube page because I am so proud of their accomplishments. They have taken the principles that I teach and put in the work to achieve their financial dreams.

Kimone Campbell worked in Corporate America for 12 to 14 hours daily on a cruise line before becoming a business owner. She had always been interested in real estate investments, buying properties, having a passive, creating a steady income with a dream to travel the world. She and I met at one of my seminars, and she was noticeably quiet and observant, paying close attention to what I was saying. Afterward, she signed up to work with me in my real estate coaching program, and soon after, she transitioned to becoming a full-time business owner.

Kimone is the owner of ADASA Properties and is now a very successful entrepreneur. She is one of the most successful people that I've come across in the past few years. What I like most about Kimone is her tenacity and drive to succeed against the odds. Not only did she apply the concepts I taught and worked really hard at it, but she also applied them during the beginning of Covid as the world was shutting down. Two days before the premiere of her Air Bnbs in Orlando, Florida, the country shut down, and everything that she planned was challenged.

Just one year after my program, she now manages three Air Bnb properties, and she wholesales properties. She has also received business funding and has signed with a real estate company. She has even earned her real estate license. She did all of this in one year. While the world was panicking, she was silently building. Instead of falling into a negative mindset, she continued to practice and push towards achieving the goals on her vision board.

Her road to success wasn't easy. She talks about having to block the naysayers and doubters that questioned why she would invest in my program. As I have said time and time again, it is normal for people to doubt you when you decide to live a life of abundance and freedom. They'll want to keep you where they are, but don't let that hinder you.

Below is a part of Kimone's testimony:

"Since I was 20, I've been starting businesses with different partners. I have a Master's, and in college, I learned a lot, and it really developed me as a person. But the really grit of it you learn from somebody else who's done it and do it well. To me, investing in myself was a no-brainer."

Today Kimone is a Master Coach in my Real Estate program. She is a testament that you will receive the fruits of your labor if you put in the work.

It's Your Time

This is the time in our journey together when I encourage you to fly your wings and soar. I am so excited that you have decided to take control of your life by creating a business that you are passionate about and can serve others. Remember that along the journey to millionaire status, you will grow into the person you see in your visions. So go back and read the questions throughout this book and read the millionaire secrets until you can commit them to memory. They will help you along the way.

When I started this journey, sometimes it was scary, and I didn't know what I was doing, but I did the work to grow my inner self. I did the work to become the person I was destined to be. And I don't think I am any different from you, so if I can do it, so can you.

Despite any obstacle you may face in your business, you should never quit. If it is what you want, it's yours. What you should stop doing is thinking that you should quit or thinking that becoming a success is not for you. Instead, you should quit the resistance to it and receive it. If you think it, it's yours – it's already yours.

I hope you have learned some valuable insights to help you on your road to becoming a thriving business owner. Our world has changed vastly over the last year, and with the pandemic that swept nation and threatened our economy, I believe it taught entrepreneurs how strong they really are. I believe it caused entrepreneurs to assess whether they can withstand the storms that will arise. There will always be adversities in life and business, and many of them will be out of our control. Don't allow adversities to slow you down. I want you to remember that there are always opportunities in obstacles. The entrepreneurs that stand firm and keep going will usually rise to the top. Successful entrepreneurs find a way or make a way. If you focus on your goals, stay positive and do things that others won't do in time of distress, you will find success like my students have had.

If you know that you want more help on this journey, my team and I are here to help you reach your goals. I would love to help you achieve your dreams because You Deserve Success!

TO YOUR SUCCESS

Get Noelle's Express Business Builder Course at
www.expressbizbuilder.com

ACKNOWLEDGEMENT

I want to thank my team of millionaires and future millionaires. I appreciate every single one of you and everything you have done to help me run these multi-million dollar businesses. I could not have done all of this without you.

ABOUT THE AUTHOR

Noelle Randall, MPS, MBA, is an Entrepreneur, Real Estate Investor, Author, Speaker, and all-around leader who is here to help!

Noelle is all about growth. She has been a thriving entrepreneur for over 20 years and is a successful businesswoman, renowned children's author, and real-estate entrepreneur. Her diverse business experience has been instrumental in her personal success as well as the success of countless people across the country.

She teaches real estate investing to women from varying backgrounds who are ready to transform their financial status. Noelle is a full-time real estate investor and founder of the Women Who Win in Real Estate Coaching Program. She provides training, workshops and hosts events to teach how to start from scratch and build a successful real estate investing business.

As CEO of Noelle Randall Coaching, Noelle offers entrepreneurs business opportunities, allowing hundreds to create wealth and financial independence through her mentorship. She has also created the opportunity to become an owner of properties across the country and obtain passive income with her company Nuurez Inc. Through her work in Nuurez, Noelle is taking the home-sharing economy to the next level! She is also the Executive Director of the Marley Simms Foundation, a public, non-profit organization dedicated to promoting children's literacy. Its mission is to advance the diversity of thought in children by providing access and awareness to books from diverse authors and discussing diverse topics.

Noelle is the founder and president of FDR Horizon Enterprises, a private real estate equity firm, and brand manager. The company owns a diverse portfolio of real estate and has created numerous profitable and top-selling brands, including her signature product, Tea More Skinny (TeaMoreSkinny.com). In addition, Noelle is the co-founder of Bella J Hair (BellaJHair.com), the premier virgin hair extension brand and international hair and wig distributor.

In addition to being a tenacious entrepreneur and businesswoman, Noelle considers herself a perpetual student, always learning and growing. Noelle proudly boasts two advanced degrees. She earned her Bachelor's Degree from the University of Connecticut in Urban Planning. She has a Master's Degree in Economic Development from Penn State, and most recently, she earned a Master's in Business Administration (MBA) from Baylor University.

Noelle is also the proud mother of seven children, whom she credits as her inspiration for every endeavor.

"To reach a new level of success in what you do, you should learn all about that one thing, do it and become an expert. Once you are an expert, you can monetize something that already makes you money!"
- Noelle Randall

CONNECT WITH NOELLE

Noelle Randall, MPS, MBA, is an engaging, transparent, and powerful speaker for audiences wishing to learn real estate and live the lives they have always wanted.

Noelle is always willing to help and teach new methods and techniques to those who might actually need them. She incorporates her teachings into her life. She does not hesitate to educate people about the secrets to becoming a millionaire in real estate. Her goal is to help and make more people become millionaires like herself.

Noelle is devoted to helping more people, and she can be sought through her website *www.noellerandall.com* or her social media accounts:

facebook.com/noellerandallcoaching

https://twitter.com/noelle_randall

https://www.instagram.com/noellerandallcoaching/

https://youtube.com/c/noellerandall1

contact@noellerandall.com